THE KEENER SIDE:

A BIBLE PROFESSOR'S TOTALLY RIGHTEOUS HUMOR

CRAIG S. KEENER

GLOSSAHOUSE WILMORE, KY

WWW.GLOSSAHOUSE.COM

GH

THE KEENER SIDE:
A BIBLE PROFESSOR'S TOTALLY RIGHTEOUS HUMOR

© GlossaHouse, LLC, 2017

GlossaHouse, LLC
110 Callis Circle
Wilmore, KY 40309
www.GlossaHouse.com

ISBN-13: 978-1942697466

Interior design by Fredrick J. Long
Cover design by T. Michael W. Halcomb

Dedicated to Bible Students
Everywhere
(especially those who are
required to take my classes).

All royalties due to me will be
donated to the scholarship funds
of Langham Partnership to help
equip scholar-leaders.

IDEAS FOR CORRELATING COMICS
TO SCRIPTURAL PASSAGES

A NOTE FROM THE AUTHOR: HERE ARE SOME VERSES WHERE TEACHERS WANTING TO INJECT A LITTLE HUMOR INTO THEIR CLASS COULD USE THESE CARTOONS. THE VERSES THEMSELVES ARE NOT MEANT TO BE FUNNY, BUT SOMETIMES ONE CAN USE HUMOR TO RELAX STUDENTS BEFORE LAUNCHING INTO THE SERIOUS MEANING OF THE PASSAGES.

12: Dorita for the foot-washing: John 13:14.

15: Akkadian Worship Language: 1 Cor 12-14

19: Baptism and roof repairs: Mark 1:5; John 4:1; Acts 2:41; 1 Cor 1:13-17; etc.

20: Thief and robber: John 10:1

26: Different sort of stocks and bonds: Matt 24:9; Acts 16:24; Rom 8:18; 1 Cor 4:12; 2 Tim 3:12; 1 Pet 1:6; Rev 12:11; etc.

27: Hammurabi's "I for an i": Exod 21:24; Lev 24:20; Deut 19:21; Matt 5:38

31: Lot's wife: Gen 19; Lev 16:8; Josh 18:6-10; 1 Sam 14:42; 1 Chron 24:31; Neh 10:34; Luke 17:32; Acts 1:26; etc.

41: Uncircumcised Philistines: Judg 14:3; 1 Sam 14:6; 17:26, 36; 1 Chron 10:4; etc.

46: Wife's anniversary: Prov 5:18; 18:22; 19:14; 31:10; verses about remembering

47: Church planting: 1 Cor 3:6

48: Moses hailing: Exod 9:18-34

51: Midwife: Gen 35:17; 38:28; Exod 1:15-21

52: Ed and Helen: Rom 15:2; 1 Cor 10:23; 14:3-26; Eph 4:29

53: Well-grounded hamburger: Luke 15:23; Eph 3:17; Col 1:23

54: Imitation and flattery: 1 Cor 4:16; 11:1; 1 Thess 1:6; 2:5; 2 Thess 3:7, 9; Heb 13:7

62: Calvinists get elected: Matt 24:22; Mark 13:20; Luke 18:7; Rom 8:33; Tit 1:1

66: Fan mail: Prov 15:4; 25:15; Luke 6:26; Rom 2:29; 1 Cor 4:5; 11:2; Eph 4:29

67: Doctrinal watchdog: Job 30:1; Matt 7:15; John 13:34-35; 17:21; Acts 20:28-29; Eph 4:31; Phil 3:2; Col 3:8; Rev 2:2, 4

68: Hot sauce preacher: Jer 20:9; Acts 18:24; 2 Tim 1:6

69: Seminarians lobby for recess: Exod 20:10; Mark 6:31

71: Professor Modassi and exams: Matt 7:13-14; 1 Cor 4:5; 1 John 4:17; etc.

74: Church bouncers at friendly church: John 13:34; Rom 15:7

76: Head pastor, pastoring the body: Acts 20:28; Rom 12:4-5; 1 Cor 12:22-25; Col 2:19

77: Pastor McNeal's blanket condemnation: Acts 20:9

79: Middle-aged pastor: 1 Tim 5:1-2; 1 Pet 5:5

84: Hippo-critters: Matt 6:2; 23:13; Mark 7:6; 12:15; Luke 6:42; 12:1, 56; 13:15; Gal 2:13; 1 Tim 4:2; 1 Pet 2:1

87: Prof's memory card: Mark 8:18; Acts 20:35; Rom 15:15; Heb 10:32; 2 Pet 3:2; Jude 17; Rev 3:3

90: Dismembered: Matt 18:17; 1 Cor 5:5; 2 Thess 3:6; 1 Tim 1:20

93: Beefs up security: Neh 4:13; Jonah

96: Theological conundrums: Mark 8:17-18; John 3:4; 2 Thess 2:10

98: Snake Handling Pastor: Mark 16:9-20

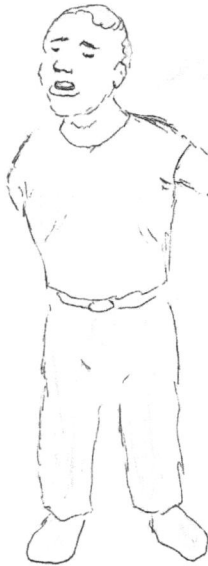

WHY WE DO STAFF TRAINING

CHRISTIAN ELEMENTARY SCHOOL STUDENTS LISTEN ATTENTIVELY TO THE NEW BASIC ENGLISH TRANSLATION OF THE BIBLE.

Class, let's continue our reading in Acts 1:18, "Judas splattered and all his guts came out ..."

SEEKING TO BECOME MORE RELEVANT, FIRST CHURCH UPDATES BIBLICAL COMMANDMENTS...

Thou shalt:

Be nice to your pet
Recycle
Eat organic
Vote green

Thou shalt not:

Give the middle finger
Enable codependency
Text while driving
Fall behind on Facebook
Eat junk food
Draw unfunny cartoons

BREAKING NEWS: KING JAMES BIBLE INSTITUTE fires PROFESSOR SHORT FOR SHOWING SEMI-NUDE PHOTO OF HIS DOG.

(What's wrong with you? Don't look!!!!)

CUSTODIAN "CLEANLINESS-IS-NEXT-TO-GODLINESS" HARRY
AND PROFESSOR "ORGANIZED-CHAOS" JEFFREY
GET INTO A FISTFIGHT OVER JEFFREY'S OFFICE

FREEZING DURING HIS MIDTERM, LARRY STRUGGLES TO REMEMBER WHO WROTE "PAUL'S LETTER TO THE ROMANS."

Hmm

DETERMINED TO MAKE THE U.S. FALL, ITS
ENEMIES CUT OFF THE CAFFEINE SUPPLY.

*To make sure her friends get a **SPECIAL** spiritual blessing, Dorita goes without showering for a week before the foot-washing service.*

The relativist, yet Anselmian, pupil challenges the old-fashioned, neofoundationalist teacher's denial of Super-Doggie.

Species-ist! Historicist! Existence-ist! Potentiality must inform ontology!

A SAD DAY IN REFORMATION HISTORY: HULDRYCH ZWINGLI DISCOVERS THAT, BECAUSE OF MERE DISAGREEMENT OVER THE LORD'S SUPPER, MARTIN LUTHER HAS UNFRIENDED HIM ON FACEBOOK. ☹

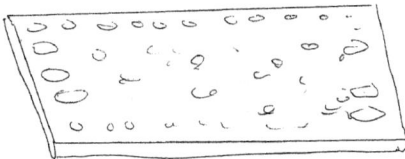

where in the world did
I put my glasses?!!

Annoyed by his parishioners' resistance to baptism, the pastor refuses their proposed roof repairs ...

AFTER SEEING THAT PHILIP PERFORMS <u>REAL</u> MIRACLES, SIMON MAGUS SUES HIS SEMINARY FOR DEFECTIVE PREPARATION.

ON THE FIRST DAY OF CLASS, PROFESSOR
MARTIN DECIDES THAT SHE'S GOING TO HAVE
TO HAVE A TALK WITH THE ADMISSIONS OFFICE

HUMAN BEANS ...

ETHICALLY QUESTIONABLE GENETIC HYBRIDS?

"YOU ARE WHAT YOU EAT"

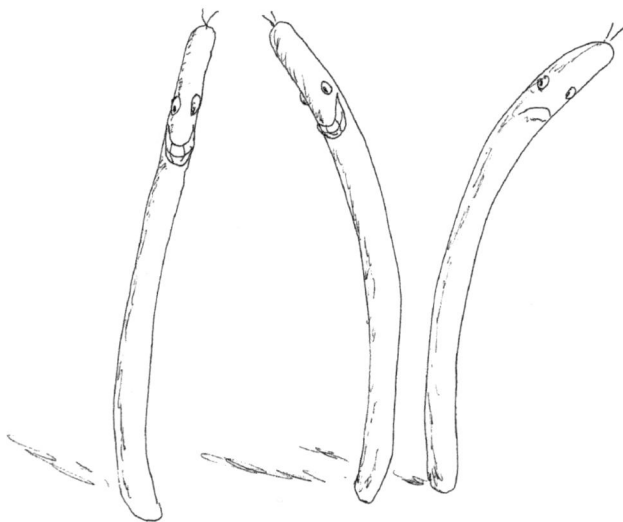

Pythagoras would have said, "I told you so."

On the Roman festival of Saturnalia, waitresses and flight attendants get to tell customers what they **really** think of them.

ALTHOUGH ONCE EXPELLED FROM SEMINARY FOR PLAGIARISM, TOBY BECOMES A FAMOUS AUTHOR, WRITING PILGRIM'S PROGRESS, THE CHRONICLES OF NARNIA, THE AUTOBIOGRAPHY OF BENJAMIN FRANKLIN, AND THE KING JAMES VERSION OF THE BIBLE.

GUILTY-LOOKING PASTOR CAUGHT NEXT TO TOPLESS BAR

After years of complaints from faculty about wearing hot Medieval dresses as graduation robes, the Graduation Company devises a more stylish and less expensive way to dress.

No matter what, the new campus postal worker is determined to get Dr. Smith-Waddell's 100 copies of her new book into her campus mailbox.

HARVEY ALWAYS HAS THE ANSWER ON THE TIP OF HIS TONGUE.

Immersed in his Old Testament assignments, Egbert temporarily forgets his surroundings

WARNED THAT HE WILL SOON BE FIRED FOR HIS INTELLECTUAL INCOMPETENCE, PROFESSOR WATKINS DEMONSTRATES HIS MENTAL AGILITY BY GRABBING A FIRE EXTINGUISHER.

BY EXPLAINING ESTHER AS AN ALLEGORY OF
QUANTUM PHYSICS, "CUTTING-EDGE" JIM WINS
THE NATIONAL ARTFORD POSTGRADUATE AWARD
IN CREATIVE INTERDISCIPLINARY THOUGHT.

CLASS HAS BEEN SO MUCH MORE FUN FOR BILL SINCE HE GOT EARBUDS FOR HIS *i*PHONE.

SEMINARIANS SOMETIMES STRUGGLE TO UNDERSTAND BIBLICAL CULTURE.

READING THE BIBLE FOR THE FIRST TIME, ED IS PLEASED TO DISCOVER THAT GOD WANTS EVERYBODY TO BE LIKE ED, WHEREAS HIS WIFE HELEN IS RELEGATED TO A FOOTNOTE.

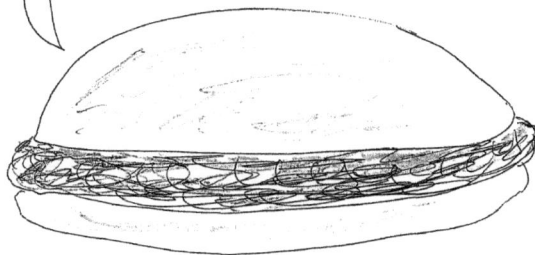

Informed that the article he plagiarized was written by his Professor, the student argues that imitation is the highest form of flattery ...

To his amazement, Professor Petrie discovers the original biblical autographs.

At last, the origin-of-life specialist discovers the elusive primordial soup.

Having met online, this couple finds that screen time with each other remains their favorite part of their marriage.

EARLY CHRISTIANS AVOIDED AMPHITHEATERS BECAUSE OF BLOODSHED THERE. TERTULLIAN TOLD OF A CHRISTIAN WOMAN WHO WENT ANYWAY AND HAD TO HAVE DEMONS CAST FROM HER AFTERWARDS..

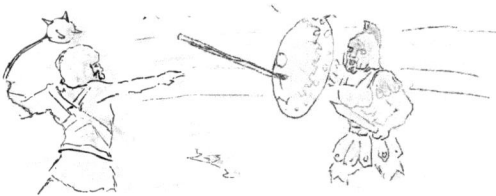

MID-TWENTIETH CENTURY CONSERVATIVE EVANGELICALS AVOIDED MOVIE THEATERS, CONCERNED ABOUT SEX AND VIOLENCE

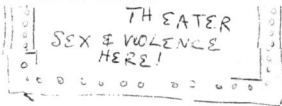

PROGRESSIVE TWENTY-FIRST CENTURY EVANGELICALS WATCH IT IN THEIR LIVING ROOMS.

Oh, cool. did you see that Monster rip that lady's guts out?

In the School parking lot Dean Ribbons confirms student reports that Professor Gray is near-sighted.

A STRONG PREDESTINARIAN, PROFESSOR RALPHIE SAVES TIME BY CALCULATION OF GRADES BEFORE THE SEMESTER BEGINS.

Hey hey hey

A TRUE BIBLICAL STUDIES GEEK

NOW THAT THE HOT SUMMER VACATION HAS ARRIVED,
THE DEPARTMENT HEAD FINALLY OPENS HER FAN MAIL.

What a fiery preacher!
Naw, man, I get like that too when I eat hot sauce.

SEMINARIANS LOBBY FOR RECESS

Give me a break!

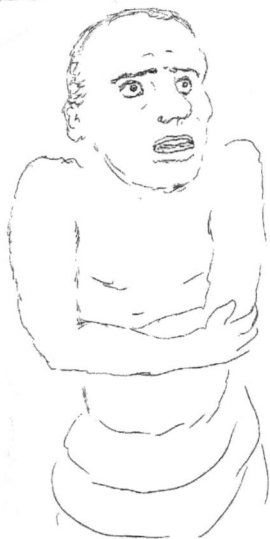

Now even the cafeteria provides methodical theological instruction.

Give thanks for precisely 25 minutes, then next eat your veggies, then...

RAPTURE HELMETS NOW AVAILABLE
AT A DISCOUNTED PRICE

... IN CASE YOU'RE INSIDE A BUILDING WHEN THE RAPTURE TAKES PLACE.

ONLY $12.95!

BUT NO DEFERRED PAYMENTS INTO THE MILLENNIUM. (SPECIAL SALE AFTER THE START OF THE GREAT TRIBULATION)

ALSO AVAILABLE: RAPTURE ROOF INSURANCE

... IN CASE YOU DAMAGE YOUR ROOF BY EXITING DURING THE RAPTURE.

(TRIBULATION DAMAGE INSURANCE NOT INCLUDED.)

CHURCH BOUNCERS

ALTHOUGH PEOPLE FALL ASLEEP IN CHURCH FOR
DIFFERENT REASONS, PASTOR MCNEAL OFFERS A
BLANKET CONDEMNATION OF THE PRACTICE.

DR. FEASEWALTER DISCOVERS WHAT THE ADVERTISER MEANT BY "COMPLIMENTARY" DRINKS.

Some Hermeneutical Movements

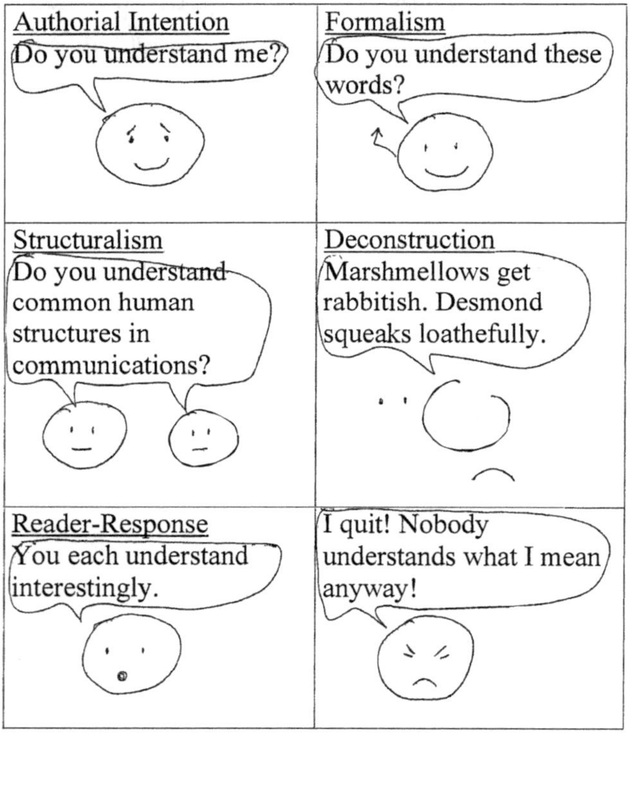

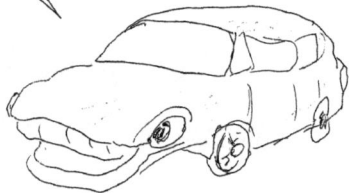

No theology intended. This is merely a CARtoon.

ALTHOUGH HAPPY AND HILDA ATTEND FIRST CHURCH,
EVERYONE KNEW THAT THEY WERE HIPPO-CRITTERS.

Unable to secure a teaching position by more conventional methods, Ralph hires a marketing firm to promote him near the campus.

WITHOUT THE PROPER GEOMETRY PREREQUISITES, STUDENTS PROVE UNABLE TO MASTER THE WESLEYAN QUADRILATERAL.

But Professor, in our first course we never got past triangles!

AFTER SIX MONTHS OF NECK PAIN, ALFRED FINALLY LOCATES HIS MISSING HAMMER IN HIS PILLOWCASE.

And I thought my teachers were the pain in my neck...

THE SEMINARY BEEFS UP SECURITY.

No, the syllabus said, "Due Date," NOT "DO Date"!
I guess that means I can't date anymore ... ?

SOME APPARENT THEOLOGICAL CONUNDRUMS ARE LIKE THIS.

Arriving in heaven, the snake-handler discovers, to his dismay, that Mark 16:18 was merely a later interpolation.

Shoot! All that handlin' for nothin' ....

So, work hard on your text criticism.